THE BOOK OF NEBIA

An Original Practice fantasy play in 3 acts.

THE BOOK OF NEBIA
[*An Original Practice fantasy play in three acts.*]

by

J.L. Davis

Characters
[*In order of appearance.*]

Shoram: A fierce warrior.
Sultina **Cossania**: Leader of Seventh Clan.
Pashil: A warrior and a hunter of the Seventh Clan.
Keeper **Lynette:** Keeper of the Seventh Clan.
Safeera: An orphan with a secret lineage.
Rashtu: A warrior-priest descended from *Nebia*.
Nebia: A young woman from ancient times.
Harat: Nebia's father, a priest.

Performers playing Rashtu/Harat should double as the veiled warriors in prologue.

This play is written to be performed outdoor or indoor on scrolls with a single text session and minimal group rehearsals (Original Practice Shakespeare style), OR fully produced per modern standards.

Original Practice Guidelines and General Notes are provided at the end of the script for any who wish to reference them.

Prologue

[Sounds of battle.]
[Enter veiled male warrior. Enter Shoram, similarly veiled.]

Sho. I swore I spied a sneaky little snake escape and skirt the border of our line. Thy blood shall soon be soak'd up by the desert sand, befouling it until the end of time.

[They fight. The man is wounded. Enter second veiled male warrior. Shoram fights him and he is also wounded, but she is stabbed in the back by the first warrior in the process. The male warriors stagger off in retreat. Shoram slumps to her knees in pain.]

[Enter the Sultina.]
Sul. My moon! What wound has caus'd thee here to fall?
Sho. *[Removes veil.]* 'Tis but an inconvenience, that is all. *[Stands in pain.]* A stark reminder to dispatch one foe before another takes thee in their thrall.
Sul. The blood is bad enough that I must ask thy service in a more important task.
Sho. I never should have ventur'd from thy side, and shall not do so hence.
Sul. Save thee thy pride, I will abide no disobedience. I order thee away unto our hold, make ready there to have our hist'ry told.

[Enter Pashil at a run.]
Pash. Sultina! *Shoram*! Who now is in command?
Sul. I am!
Sho. Our forces they are far too much entrench'd, and I would not abandon thee or them.
Sul. We'll make one final feint to drive them back, then sprint for safety after we attack. Fail not to put the guard on high alert, else their arrival cause us further hurt. We leave the field this way and live to fight these foes another day. Now go *Shoram,* whilst thou still can.
Sho. If my Sultina does command-
Sul. She does. Fear not that I shall see thee soon.
Sho. See that thou do; for thy death is my one and final doom. Watch over her *Pashil*.
Pash. I swear to thee I will.
[Exit Shoram]

Sul. (Attack! Attack!) *[To Pashil.]* Make ready to retreat along the back. I'll to the front once more to lend my strength, and when I give the signal we will all fly from this hellish place.
[Exeunt.]

Push back, attack with everything thou can! For *Nebia* and the Seventh Clan!
[Sounds of battle slowly fade.]

Act I

[*Enter Safeera, skipping and humming a tune.*]
[*Safeera stops, looks around in bewilderment, has completely forgotten what she has come to do.*]

[*Enter Keeper Lynette with two brooms–or scrolls.*]
Keep. Someday *Safeera* thou shalt be alone,
Unless thyself some blessed focus find,
[*Hands Safeera a broom, or her scroll if Original Practice.*]
As shifting sand surrounds our desert home
So roam those grains of thought within thy mind.
Saf. Good Mistress Keeper, may we make some
custards? The camels gave such milk that keeping fresh,
'til from the fortress in the Eastern mounts our folk
return, will be impossible, besides tis better fresh as thou
thyself did teach when I was but a little girl.
Keep. When but thou wast a little girl indeed.
Saf. Oh please?
We've all the sugar butter salt and eggs,
With flour enough to stand a mighty siege,
And if the custards keep till they return,
As I assure you some of them may do,
Well, who would not with strongest longing yearn
to pleasantly return to fresh confections, wouldn't you?
'Tis such a long trek home, near one full day,
Our brave Sultina, even she herself,
returning saddle sore, her backside rack'd with pain,
would praise thy name to find a dainty on the shelf.

Keep. How wouldst thou know, most whimsical of
wards, whom treats with trouble as thou had accords,
what lies within the mind of our Sultina?
Saf. She may have caught me late one winter's eve, my
hand within the pantry where my sleeve did snag upon a
nail as she approach'd, and she then my predicament
reproach'd; as I had plac'd the wayward nail that
thwarted my escape! But then I ask'd her rather
pointedly, why in the kitchen did she come alone, with
servants plentiful to fill her needs, so sneaking like a thief
in her own home?
Keep. Oh tell me thou didst not my willful child.
Saf. To tell thee I didst not would be a lie, to lie, as thou
hast told me many times, would be a sin.
Keep. Do I dare ask what happen'd then?
Saf. 'You mind your manners child', she did say. 'If
minded I my manner's', did say I, 'then mold would soon
appear upon this pie'. For I, with wisdom of one taught
that 'waste is not for those who fear to ever want', had
had mine eye upon that pie some time. Didst not thou
teach me this same worthy quote?
Keep. Forgive me if I did, by perfect wrote.
Saf. 'I notic'd deep neglect of this fair dish', so told her I
my tone most serious, 'and so to use what else might go
to waste, here came I by to save this pie; care for a taste?'
Keep. And what, pray tell these wretched ears of mine,
replied our fair Sultina to your crime?
Saf. She seem'd to think on it a goodly while,
Then sat she on a cushion was nearby,
She pointed to a cleanly looking tile,
And motion'd me to bring to her the pie.
'Physicians tell me not to eat so late',
Confided she to me as to a friend,
When I did place the pie upon its plate,
'To hell with my physicians,' said she then.

'Tell no one of our late night gluttony,
And I'll not scold thee as I surely should,
Sit thee by me and we'll the judges be
If that poor wasting pie is any good.'
Keep. So in the quiet hours of the night, when thou shouldst have been fast asleep in bed, in place of punishing, which would be right, the leader of our clan, our guiding light, sat down and shar'd a pie with thee instead?
Saf. To share implies an equal part to both, whereas to her most certain went the most.
Keep. Speak thee no ill of thy Sultina child, who could have had thee scrubbing pots for days, but rather opted to reward thy guile, by honoring thy disrespectful ways. If only I had known-
Saf. Fear not, my friend and greatest confidante, I swore to her I wouldn't tell a soul.
Keep. A promise that thou even now uphold.
Saf. So may we make the custards?
Keep. I misspoke.
Those grains of thought return quite fast enough
To focus on a treat thou truly want,
Such things as sweets it seems keep them in place;
'Tis not till talk of chores they wander off.
First let us sweep the halls of this our hold, we don't desert our duty for mere whim, and then we'll to the kitchen, I suppose; a craving I have had for cinnamon.
Saf. My mother had she liv'd to see me cry could not have had a kinder soul than thine.
Keep. Oh cherish child that rose within thy cheeks,
That smile of thine so sweet to melt a heart,
For one day I shall learn to say thee 'no',
And thou'lt be forc'd to find more clever art.

[Enter Shoram.]

Sho. A space, a space, 'gainst death of day they race,
To claim that which our clan did liberate,
From hidden vault in holy temple took,
Preserv'd in time for us to find; the book.
Keep. The book?
Sho. The hidden book of *Nebia*.
Keep. By sacred Toran's painful crown it has been
found?
Sho. No time to celebrate.
Keep. Of course, your wounds they cry for help. [*To
Safeera*.] Fetch water, clean rags, cushions for the floor:
go now.
[Exit Safeera.]

Sho. And bread: some ale if you can find it!
Keep. What circumstance begot thy injury?
Blood covers thee from mussed crown to foot,
Here let me see-
Sho. But let it be! To poke at it won't do it any good.
I'll live, or else pass on to what's beyond;
And woe to foes who wait to hinder those
Who newly to that deathly realm have come.
Yet of important matters must I speak,
Ere earthly lips are stopp'd by death or sleep.
As sure you know the purpose of our quest,
That daughter most belov'd of our Sultina,
That girl we watch'd within our hold to grow,
She that whom all of us might call our own,
And she whose laugh could fill a hundred halls,
Whose echo still resounds within these walls.
Keep. *Cozette*, our dear *Cozette*.
Sho. Even she.
We took her to the meeting of the clans,
As must we by the law that men did make,
With heavy hearts to hand her to a man,

Upon her fourteenth nameday, such her fate,
To binded be for all eternity
To victor of a contest; a trophy.
Should fail we in this antiquated rite,
Refusing to relinquish their fair prize,
The other clans would gather for a fight,
To right a grievous insult in their eyes.
So took that child we did to yonder hold,
Where all eight clans together come to meet,
And shoulders bare as in those days of old
In contest for her hand they did compete.
Yet even as the battles would unfold,
All eyes with fixed focus on the match,
As crimson wash'd upon that stony ground,
As lusty cheers for blood in throats rang out,
Our agents working in the temple depths
Sent word the Book of *Neb'ia* had been found.
Then quiet as the movements of the moons,
Unseen as in the day when they do hide
And slip from space to space within the sky,
Away slipp'd we with our unhappy bride.
Keep. Our sweet *Cozette*, oh precious girl.
Did not resistance follow thee at once?
Sho. The guards outside the grounds and at the stalls,
Where waited armed women with our mounts,
We slew as not to let them sound alarm,
And flew us fast and far upon our route.
Our train departed near the highest peak
Of that cruel sun set looming in the sky,
A half days ride at least the journey takes,
Through dunes and draws, the air too hot to cry.
Ere half again tween zenith of that sun
And blessed cooling time of moonlit night,
As briefly walk'd ourselves to spare our mounts,
Came angry shouts, as though to spur a fight.

So turn'd we swift as o're a rise they came,
And greeted them our shafts with deadly aim.
None made it to the valley floor alive,
But more, grown wise, had stopp'd atop the rise.
Keep. Their lives they owe for all the girls before,
Those lost unto our clan forevermore.
Sho. But more, and brace thee blessed *Keeper*.
Before those men slid down upon the dune,
To die a death that long they have deserv'd,
Some few did find the wherewithal to raise
Those short bows meant for mounted war; and more,
Their shots though wild one did strike a mark;
Still more, *Cozette*, whom risk'd we all our lives
To stay from most unhappy slavery,
An arrow through her tender throat did take.
Keep. Did live she on?
Then suffer'd she not long?
Sho. With but a moments shock and little pain, her
skewer'd body slip'd onto the sand, and ne'r did rise
again.
Keep. What others fell upon that cursed spot?
What names that in the past have bles'd mine ears
Must now we carve in stone, else be forgot?
What smiles here before, will light these darken'd
hallways nevermore?
Sho. No others lost we there upon that ground,
Though wish I would that skirmish were the last,
But as we near'd what refuge here is found,
They caught us less prepar'd; and there we clash'd.
So many fell a league or less from here,
To list them all would be impossible,
And many more have surely fallen now,
Deaths vengeance seeming nigh unstoppable.
Still rag'd the battle when my wounds I took,
On both sides freely flow'd life's vital blood,

A fight to make the faithful feel forsook,
Decided not, though came they like a flood,
A tide that flow'd but never fully ebb'd,
Their forces were an ocean with no end,
And on they march'd across their recent dead,
Replacing ev'ry man who fell with ten.
Keep. And our Sultina? Oh tell me that she lives!
Sho. Herself it was who sent me from the fray,
And spurr'd me on to swiftly reach our hold,
That I might ready make a quiet space,
And see that spears await our foes approach.
Astride her mount she was the last I saw,
As I ascended mine to ride away,
Her silhouette a beacon to us all
As night began to slowly steal the day.

[*Shouts without.*]

Methinks that sound announces those who live.
Keep. *Safeera*, oh that wayward girl, what shiny bauble
caught the light of lamps reflection so to stray her from
her chore. We must not have the mistress come to find
there no reception in her hall. I shall return forthwith.
[*Exit Keeper.*]

[*Enter Rashtu.*]
Sho. You! [*Draws blade and puts it to Rashtu's neck.*]
Rashtu.
How brazenly you burst into our hold,
As though a hero bent on saving us
From forces out of your benign control.
But I am not naive as others are,
Believing correspondence from afar.
What reason would a priest within the ranks
Of our oppressive enemies from birth,

Give guidance that might gain our grateful thanks
For giving us a gift of greatest worth?
'Twas you who first inform'd us of this book,
It's whereabouts, how many wards without,
And even of the time it should be took.
Alarm was sounded moments after we,
Who trusted your assessment of escape,
Did find the prize intended fatefully
That might we persecuted liberate.
Rash. It was not I who sounded the alarm,
A possibility I warn'd about,
The last thing I would wish is cause thee harm,
For my life was made forfeit at that shout.
Sho. So say you with my blade against your throat,
No longer resting safely with your kin,
Among your precious tombs the ancients wrote,
Surrounded by a sea of warlike men.
In this our hold, ther'd be no inquiry
Were I to slay a man who lay his hands on me.
Rash. I never would endeavor such a thing,
Thy words would only serve to cheapen thee,
It goes against the nature of my being
To take a lover uninvitedly.
Sho. So many have been rap'd o're centuries
By men who do precisely as they please,
Were I to fabricate one injury,
The scales would still be tilted woefully.
If one inverted justice were so met,
What saintly soul would thy demise lament?

[*Enter the Sultina, Pashil with a box wrapped in cloth.*]
Sul. Why threaten thee my moon our newfound friend?
Sho. What friend would so endanger us my love? Was it
not strange how quickly they were mounted in pursuit?
And on our heels when barely we began upon our route?

What stealthy plan with good intent so quickly yields
deployment of six independent armies to the field?
Sul. Those Sultans long have long'd for our demise, but
patient waiting on the perfect time to strike. We knew the
risk, and any of a thousand wand'ring eyes might swift
had spied a single article amiss. A sentry missing from
his post: the absence of Cozette's resplendent presence
from our host: an awkward look upon a maiden's brow as
she herself exus'd, a thousand subtle clues rebellion
brew'd beyond the masks of docile maidens in disguise
we use'd. And too what witnesses escap'd our view? A
sultan's loyal serving girl who notic'd us depart: a priest
whose bonds they found a way to fray: a stable boy left
hiding in the liv'ry yard, a hundred ways we may have
gave ourselves away. *Rashtu* is true, as all his actions
prove, in perfect concert with his promises.
Sho. How knowest thee that he is not some spy?
Sul. For reasons that he shall himself impart forthwith; a
challenge if he were to die.
Sho. I only meant to frighten a confession out of him.
[*Removes her blade from Rashtu's neck.*] Forgive me, my
Sultina, trust wears thin.
Sul. As should it in a world contriv'd by men.
Yet this one risk'd for us his life and limb,
For this *Rashtu* has earn'd our greatest trust.
In heated battle fought he by our side,
Against his very clan, by mine own eyes.
'Gainst brothers known by him since childhood,
With steel on steel he prov'd his word was good.
My life I owe his deeds upon the field.
Rash. And my life thine, the sword that thou dost wield
like lightning flash'd from corners of mine eyes, so
swiftly my would-be assassins died.
Sho. [*Sheathes blade.*] Again, I see he is not foe but
friend.

Rash. I cast no stones for thoughts thou may'st have had.
Sho. [*Reaching for blade again*.] And I care not what
thoughts that-

[*Enter Keeper, Safeera*.]
Keep. Oh! Oh! Oh!
Sul. Rise woman. Rise. How canst thou keep a hold if
holding back thy howls proves overmuch? For sake of all
that's real I beg thee rise. Distribute here those comforts
thou didst bring and join with us, as much of what we
will unfold affects us all.
Keep. Forgive me fair Sultina for my tears, I weep for
what was lost to us today.
Sul. Tomorrow let us weep for yesterday,
For much have we to learn in little time,
And tears shed now may never go away.
Pashil.

[*Pashil unwraps the box and hands it to the Sultina*.]

Pash. Our holy prize, Sultina mine.
Sho. A box is all was bought by so much blood?
How does one browse the pages of a box?
Sul. The ancient knowledge of our ancestor,
Our matriarch, inside this husk does dwell,
Well hidden and forgotten in its metal shell.
Sho. Allegedly.
Sul. What else can we believe?
What else, my fearless warlike heart, Have we?
Our people teeter on extinction's brink,
In desperation did we risk our lives
To seek our history's missing link.
All women who've been lost to us before,
Each drop of blood untimely has been shed,
If little yields the pages of the book,

Then little is the honor to our dead.
When knowledge has been alter'd, lost, eras'd,
Then by necessity one must fall back on faith.
Sho. I've never put much stock in faith.
Sul. I know. [*Caresses her cheek.*] So I shall bear the
burden for us both.
[*To Rashtu.*] In preface to the words we hope when soon
Reveal'd will heal so many ancient wounds,
Tell all of us now that we've some reprieve,
The tale thou told'st me when we first did meet.
Rash. When once I came of age to know the world
As more than foolish fancy of the young,
A time did find my father to unfold
Some secrets yet unknown to our religion.
There was before the tombs of prophets past
The words of one who liv'd within the time
When first upon this world walk'd sacred *Toran*.
Though letters were forbid to females all,
A journal none-the-less was scrib'd, by woman.
Keep. *Nebia*.
Rash. So was I by my father told.
My eyes have never known what lies within,
The pages foreign to myself as thee,
Perhaps a secret since they first were penn'd,
Deliver'd now to thee by destiny.
Pash. Some whispers have there been but little more,
Small hints of heresay heard throughout our lives,
Fair fragments born on tongues but quickly hush'd.
Rash. All meant to reunite our fam'ly line.
For I am kin to *Nebia* myself,
The last male scion living at this time,
Descended of that woman from the past,
And task'd to tie my mortal fate to thine.
A key my father did present to me,
Unlocks this box lost to our family,

But kept by certain members of the church,
All whom knew not the boxes truest worth.
Of strongest metal forg'd by master smith,
They had no earthly way to open it.
Sho. And only now you chose to seek us out,
When half thy life thou knew what lie inside?
Rash. My father made me memorize a rhyme,
As did his father unto him before,
And so forth all the way from Nebia's time,
A rhyme I shall keep from the world no more:

When man commands unquestioning our race,
Upon the eve of ending ev'ry trace
Of female freedom yet in place,
A daughter born in secret shall arise
And spread a truth to end the ancient lies.

When wives and daughters are as property,
This key shall set the persecuted free.
Within a box of molten metal made,
A book of truth to rest there has been laid,
To end a nearly neverending strife,
To give to slaves the mastery of life,
The words of my most dear departed wife,
Nebia.

I cannot say exactly how I knew
When all of these conditions would come true,
But recently I felt a, heaviness,
And something in my very soul I swear
Would not give me a moment's rest
Until I saw the book deliver'd here.
Sul. Here is the box.
Rash. And here the key.

[Shouts of alarm without.]

Pash. Already they've regroup'd and reach'd our hold.
Sho. I'll go to lend my strength and soon report.
Sul. I order thee to sit before thou fall, *Pashil* is more
than capable of holding down the fort. Let everyone see
that thou come from me, to share command and bring
back word of what thou see.
Pash. Thou can depend on me, Sultina.
Saf. What army waits outside our gates?
Sho. Six armies would be more precise.
Pash. Fear not *Safeera* what awaits, oh little one whom
once I taught to hunt, our hold is well protected from the
front, with arrow slits to make intruders pay before they
even reach the metal of our gate. And then our pikes
we'll put to work to hamper all their efforts through the
grates. Then even more surprises wait them from above,
for we have plann'd against this very onslaught's
probability for months. A much concerted effort will it
take from all the Sultans' clans ere our defenses break.
Rash. And I as well would offer up my aid.
My sacred duty now has been fulfill'd,
My story told, my usefulness is done.
Thou hast the key, let me protect this hold,
My life has been a somewhat weary one.
I know the minds and tactics of these men,
There's none more suited for delaying them.
Sul. Go with our blessing then, and buy us time;
Distract them, kill them, negotiate a pause,
So make thy words be heard as they were mine,
Whatever thou must do to give us breath,
To read the words we hope will bring us life,
And see what we have bought with so much death.
Pash/Rash. Sultina.

[Exit Pashil, Rashtu.]

Sul. Let we who live bear witness to this day,
We four brave souls who represent our clan,
Who carv'd a home within this rocky hold
Where women pay no homage to a man.
Behold as we retrieve our talisman,
That we might find new strength through revelation.
Dear *Shoram*, my companion since our youth,
The world seems not itself without you near,
Where'er thou goest my heart goes with thee,
And where thou settle I will surely stay.
How proud I am to be with thee today.
Lynette, our *Keeper*, mother to our clan,
Who rais'd a willful child, don't protest,
When simplest lessons show'd me at my worst,
Thou wert most sure to teach me what was best.
How bless'd I am to be with thee today.
Safeera dear; oh yes, I know thy name.
Within thee lies the future of our clan,
The youth are whom the noble strive to help,
And hope to help do I with all I am.
How lucky we to have thee here today.
Lynette has rais'd thee with an open heart,
And tells me often of thy clever mind.
Saf. Thy words are kind, or so I do perceive; although
my focus has been question'd recently.
Keep. O' child thou dost live to torment me.
Saf. Thy Keeper claims my thoughts will wander here
and there and there and there and-
Sul. I trust that still we share a secret bond?
Saf. Of course. It is a secret I've not shar'd with anyone;
but one. Yet she will never tell for keeping is her sacred
trust, and keeping secrets simpler I would say than
keeping this place free of dust.
Keep. Almighty Thought above in whom we trust.

Sul. Forgive thee I for in thy hands it lies,
To pass along our very memory,
Our words, our deeds, the knowledge of our lives.
Since thou art youngest in this company,
I give to thee this hard begotten key,
That thou might show us where our path may lead.
Saf. Without delay I shall this box unlock, for those who find that they are under siege I think should hardly take such time to talk.
Keep. Girl…
Saf. A hole whereto insert the holy key is lacking in availability.
Sul. Its crafting was conceiv'd inside the heart,
A forge that burns beyond all mortal steels,
Which added magic to the blacksmith's art
So that to eyes alone a secret it conceals.
Saf. If only riddles swept the floor, or lifted heavy things, or open'd doors when hands were full, or really any helpful thing-
Sul. Be guided not by natural means, but by an instinct that lies lock'd inside of thee.
Sho. And hope us all inside lies what we seek.

[*Safeera closes her eyes and unlocks the box. The book slides free.*]

Saf. A journal it appears to be.

[*The Sultina takes up the book.*]

Sho. Gently.
Sul. It's binding still is strong, and not too brittle. The spine appears to separate but little. The writing on the cover's in the ancient tongue, which we were taught to translate very young.

Saf. 'Tis only fair to share for 'tis no aging pie.
Sul. [*Reads*.] *Nebia*, daughter of *Harat* and *Jezaphine*.
Keep. Almighty *Toran* keep us, protect us.
Sul. Scorches abound, darkoning the edges-
Keep. Oh save us from our sin with holy flesh-
Sul. As if someone did wish to burn it once-
Keep. Thy sacrifice protect us from ourselves-
Sul. Yet flowing script is clear in gentle strokes-
Keep. Thy mercy in our souls unholy dwells-
Sul. The authors words are easy to make out-
Keep. From deepest darkest night deliver us.
Sho. Pray to the Thoughts *Lynette*, not to a man; nor any
mascot which is masculine.
Sul.

4th day of Lunestrad, year 333 after the Split.

*I write these words in total secrecy, for none may know
that father taught my letters to me. If any find this who
would be a friend to me, then burn it down to ash
immediately. They might expel him from the church if any
knew, and so the greatest trust I place in you.
My fourteenth nameday came and went, a day that I
would just as soon forget. For father introduc'd me to a
man that I had never met, who reek'd of livestock
chewing leaf and suet. An aged fellow missing most his
hair, who eyed me as he would a...*

It's scratch'd but, 'prized mare' I think.

[Shift to past.]

[Enter Nebia.]

Neb. (A prized mare.)

Neb/Sul. [*Nebia to audience, the Sultina still reading.*] (We had some words about it in the evening.)

[*Those in the present bear silent witness to the past.*]

[*Enter Harat.*]

Neb. My blessed father *Harat* who art as the Thoughts to me, for so they daily teach, I hope the grandfather thou show'd me to was pleas'd?

Har. Do not start on me *Nebia*, he is a most important man. A deacon with a multitude of herds and large amounts of land.

Neb. What say have I, oh wise *Harat*, in dealings between men? For lowly girls are naught but property was given birth from them.

Har. Thou knowst that is not true, for thou hast read unalter'd script I know. The Thoughts inhabited both man and woman when they first did into human bodies flow.

Neb. But father wouldst we not be ston'd to speak of it?

Har. Yes. But thou art wise enough to keep thy education quiet. I will do what I can to see that elder *Hammond* not allow a match with goodman *Johan*. A certain odor hangs about that man, and by the Thoughts for thee is he quite old; with wives enough already at his hold.

Neb. Thy supper near is ready father: stew. I hope you think it good enough to feed whatever man I'm given to.

Har. Enough!

Neb. Forgive me.

Har. My precious little one. My blessed girl. The times are dark and those who lead our church grow desp'rate not to lose control.

Neb. The times do not seem dark at their majestic holds, where flowers well are tended to and water fountains flow. It seems that only in the towns is poverty and darkness found. 'Tis true as I have heard, the library at *Telanon* was burn'd?

Har. And any stone with so much as a carving smash'd by iron picks in turn.

Neb. Thou tookst us there when mother was alive. It was so beauteous, and fill'd to brimming were it's archives.

Har. Best not to mention that to anyone. Especially to *Toren*, for I know that thou art friends.

Neb. We were. He tried to force me into something that is best you do not know, and for his efforts did receive a less than subtle blow; as thou did teach me father. And I am not the first he's lur'd to a barn.

Har. Be careful child, words as those can only cause us harm. Avoid him if thou can. His father is the head of all the prophets now, and claims the boy to be immaculate, of all yet not of any man or clan.

Neb. Ha! *Toren*? Why call his father father then? Inhabited directly by the Thoughts-

Har. Thy ridicule had best not leave this house, or there will be a cost.

Neb. If anyone is blessed of the Thoughts it is the smithy boy.

Har. Young *Willimund*?

Neb. He walks me to the church when thou art gone. It keeps the other boys at bay for he is very strong. His arms are large as any full-grown man, yet inside he's as gentle as a lamb.

Har. Thou must not grow attach'd to this young man if value thee thy health and his.

Neb. He only walks me to the church.

Har. Well, that is good. He has my thanks. Unless I quickly rise within the ranks I fear I may not have a say in who dost take thy hand. The problem is, thou'rt growing faster than my standing can. But be at ease dear

one, and do not brood. I quickly must one final errand
run, and on returning we will have that stew.
[*Exit Harat.*]

[*Shift to present.*]

Keep. Blaspheme!
Sho. No Keeper, truth. At last, some truth.
Sul. Too long have we been taught a proclamation from
a priest is testament, while witness from a woman still
requires proof.
Keep. She cannot speak of *Toran* who relieves us of our
sin.
Sho. A thing is easy to relieve one of when you control
it's very definition.
Sul. These words are come directly from the one who
dipp'd the quill into the well, not to affect the thoughts
and actions of her people, but merely for she had a story
of her own to tell. Why think thee *Nebia* had to learn her
letters so covertly? Why think thee *Nebia* documents
destruction of a library? If you would weave a proper
web of lies, you must be rid of any information to the
contrary, else any flies you hope catch might choose
another path and miss your web entirely.
Sho. It is the same with sultan's who will always claim
successful raiding bands, when I myself with other sisters
of the sword and spear repell'd them from our lands with
empty hands. They long have us'd such lies to lure our
young men away with promises of great prosperity.
Keep. Well I will trust thy wisdom, both of thee, and yet
these revelations fill me with uncertainty.
Sho. Didst thou expect the truth to bring us peace, as
though a pretty picture painted by a priest?
Keep. I only mean it's hard to think a single source could
so expose such vast conspiracy. The boys we raise to men

within our hold, they are not evil things no more than we.
Could they have been so diff'rent then? Most certainly
not all of them.
Sho. If men of olden times were kind we would not find
ourselves in this predicament, where women only are
allow'd vicarious control of land or herd once they have
made a promise to obey and serve.
Keep. Forgive me for this takes some acclimation.
Sul. Thou dost not need forgiveness from thy peers.
Recovering from long enforc'd indoctrination can take
many years. Yet we have no such luxury of time in which
to find a gentle adaptation.
Keep. Well then, read more before I've further time to
think of all the implications.
Sul.

22nd day of Lunestrad, year 333 after the Split.

*Today the miller and his wife were taken from their
homes, into the central square where he was lash'd, and
she was ston'd. A metal item she, Hypalia was her name,
had fashion'd that she claim'd by monitoring movements
of the moons would navigation aid. We all were order'd
from our homes to gather and participate. I fear for
Willimund, whose father help'd to shape the metal that
she us'd.*

[Shift to past.]

Neb/Sul. *[Nebia to audience, the Sultina still reading.]*
(So far of nothing has he been accus'd.)

[Enter Harat.]

Neb. Oh father!
Har. My darling girl.

Neb. Didst thou not have a voice in these proceedings?
Har. I voted that the item be detroy'd, and she be banish'd to a monastery. I knew that any less would call to question my own piety.
Neb. Why dost thou move so gingerly? [*She lifts the back of his shirt.*]
Har. Ah!
Neb. Was this for talk of only banishment?
Har. 'Twill heal with time, do not lament.
Neb. Was any talk of punishing the smith?
Har. He wisely claim'd he had no notion what she meant to do with it. I vouch'd for him, for I know thou art fond of *Willimund*.
Neb. Was my affection for the smithy boy the reason thou wert whipp'd?
Har. I cannot say, but do not blame thyself. I made no sound and so they found it prudent to reward me. A larger room, and wider congregation too. This is a blessing in disguise for me and you.
Neb. A time there was when bones of innocents had not to break for blessings. When statesmen would have stopp'd such gross indignities. These clergymen are ruthless in their clear abuse of power.
Har. *Hypalia* knew the risk of contradicting doctrine.
Neb. How canst thou say that father? What if't were I who us'd my knowledge to construct–
Har. Do not complete that thought. I know thou never would be so inordinately reckless. Thou art the wisest girl I've ever known.
Neb. The wisest girl?
Har. The wisest child too, for such is how we educated you. I know that thou wilt find thy happiness within whatever place the church does choose for thee. Remember always though, when thy beliefs do contradict the clergy, always is it best to let the matter be.

Neb. But-
Har. I'm tir'd *Nebia*. I must to bed and early rise.
Neb. Thou hast not eaten.
Har. I fear I have no appetite. I'll eat when I do wake.
Goodnight my precious girl, my leave now I must take.
[Exit Harat.]

[Shift to present.]

Sul.

1st day of Henestro, year 334 after the Split.

I have not written in some time, but the events of late lay heavy on mind. Some weeks ago now Toren pick'd a fight with Willimund. It did not go too well for him, or for his friends who tried half-heartedly to help. And now I live in fear that-

[Enter Pashil, Rashtu.]

Pash. Forgive us for the interruption my Sultina.
Sul. Speak.
Pash. A situation has arisen that requires thy attention.
Rash. It may be possible to make a nightly peace, but first the sultans need assurances from thee. They only will begin a conversation though if thou convey thy sentiments through me.
Sho. How typically belittling.
Sul. Then let us use their arrogance against them and pretend that we are meek, considering surrender if it is surrender that they seek. A night of peace is more than I had dar'd to hope, and for such respite with a thousand of their toothless insults would I cope. The situation favors them, and yet thou hast done well in spite of it. Return to

them *Rashtu* and tell them I shall soon emerge to send my wilting woman's wishes through a manly intermediate.

[*Exit Rashtu.*]

The three of thee should find a little time for sleep. I'll send for thee when I am sure that we may unmolested be as farther on we read, and through the words of *Nebia* we'll see what she did see. *Safeera* dear, please keep this precious tomb with thee.

Saf. I'll keep it with me proudly; though the box looks rather heavy.

Keep. So tried have I to train that tongue Sultina; like trying to teach calmness to the sea.

Sul. No longer need we box and key my girl, from this day to forevermore, we here release these words into the world. May they be shouted from the mountaintops one day, that nevermore may any women by religious doctrine be enslav'd.

Sho. It would be safer for thee were I by thy side.

Sul. Dost think thy bleeding on our enemy might somehow help me in a fight? My mind would find more peace were thou to take at least an hour or two to rest. I'd join thee if I could, but duty dictates how I now may serve our people best. Fear not my loving moon, I have *Pashil*, and still a host of many loyal warriors bearing temper'd steel.

Pash. [*To Shoram.*] I swear to thee that I will give my life ere any wielded sword or spear or knife should come within a distance that might harm thy lawful wife.

Sho. Do not neglect projectiles from their bows.

Pash. Or take an arrow too if so it goes. No earthly weapon wielded by our foe that any man might swing or thrust or shoot or throw.

Sul. Now that we've settl'd that ad nauseum, let no one here feel fear for what's to come.

[*Exit Sultina, Pashil.*]

Sho. That woman is too calm for one who grieves. I fear that she replaces preservation with belief in those prophetic visions she receives. She lost a daughter only hours gone.

Keep. We all did.

Sho. I know, and now must somehow carry on. But still…

Keep. Cozette will ever live within our memory. We'll honor her with ev'ry word and ev'ry deed that leads to our Sultina's vision of our people being freed.

Sho. We are agreed. And yet whatever peace they're offering I'd scarcely trust. Exposed are they in the elements with little means to resupply, while we are comfy in our hold and so can hold out for a time if must. If I were they and thought like savage men, I'd swiftly overwhelm us in the night, before the glaring sun arose to bring the heat that comes with morning light. Before too long they will decide to try and end this fight; and we are far outnumbered.

[*Exit Shoram.*]

Saf. I do not think alone that I could sleep.

Keep. Oh child, if only for a little time, thou mayest rest with me.

[*Exeunt.*]

SUGGESTED INTERMISSION

Act II

[Enter Pashil, the Sultina from opposite sides.]

Pas. Didst find thou any rest at all?
Sul. I'll rest when all this mess has been resolv'd.
Pas. And *Shoram*?
Sul. Too weak is she to rise, though did endeavor to
convince me otherwise. Her wounds have worsen'd
through the night.
Pas. The Keeper and the girl?
Sul. Awake but slow to rise. The Keeper's hands are full
with our *Safeera*. I sense in her the spirit of our ancestors.
Pas. Sheer stubbornness more like. Forgive.
Sul. Whatever keeps her safe for she may be the last of
us, and come what may she must escape and save the
book or all that we have done will be for naught.
O'er time our line has much diminished,
Our women taken as the sultan's slaves,
Our men seduc'd by shiny promises;
We are not what we were in olden days.
Should these invaders come in all their force,
We'll send her out the hidden passageway,
That she may safe in subtle stealth escape,
While with our lives their progress we delay.
It is the only way she can be free
To carry on our long-fought legacy.
Pas. I live to serve and I shall die when thou require it
Sultina. Dost thou believe the clan chiefs mean to keep
the peace till dawn?
Sul. They pitch their tents in mock indifference,

Yet stay alert with all their armor on;
I don't believe we have much time at all.
Pas. As hunted animals will still protect their young, so I
shall stay by thy side as we fall.

[*Enter Keeper, Safeera.*]
Keep. Forgive me my Sultina for the wait.
Sul. I only hope thou found a little sleep,
To keep alert and hear *Safeera* read.
Saf. What me?
Sul. It is thy book now dear.
Saf. I thought it was a sacred tomb?
Sul. As sacred as the blessed moons, but we are *Nebia's*
remaining kin, as *Rashtu* is whom thou hast recent met.
Saf. We all are kin to *Nebia*?
Sul. We three alone. 'Tis common in the line of our
Sultina's to be bless'd by birthing twins, as I did when I
bore my dear *Cozette*. Her sister we conspir'd to
separate, that she could not be fought for in the
tournament. Thou wert that sister; and my daughter too.
Saf. Today I lost a sister that I never knew?
Keep. Thou knew her well in passing child, and she
knew you, though thou could never be the sisters that
thou may have wanted to.
Sul. Thy father was a warrior of our clan,
A handsome man with eyes the same as thine,
Who willing gave that seed of life to me
In order to advance our fam'ly line.
It was an honor so to serve said he.
Saf. Where is he then, this man who sir'd us so readily?
Sul. There was a raid one night when thou wert young,
And he among the warriors who went out,
To meet those raiders at the setting sun,
Approaching from a fortifi'd redoubt.
I came across the carnage in the night,

And in the moonlight saw that he had died.
He did acquit himself heroic'lly.
Saf. Not any word of this was told to me.
Sul. Thy freedom I felt more important than the
knowledge of thy lineage. Had one o're-hearing ear been
tied to some foolhardy tongue; that's not to say that thine
is such a one, yet foolishness may masquerade as
innocence among the young; I mean to say-
Saf. But this man knew of our *Cozzette* at birth?
Sul. He made a promise to remain aloof, and kept his
word. I do regret the need for secrecy, but ever will be
grateful for thy life as a reward.
Keep. The absence of a father's not uncommon even in
the other clans; and some are such that children would be
better off without.
Saf. I never felt such absence with so many goodly
matrons all about, nor absence of a mother I concede; our
keeper was the only mother I might ever need.
Keep. Girl!
Sul. No-no, 'tis good that she should feel this way, as I
would too. I always knew thy safety was worth more than
what forgiveness I might ask, and may make easier thy
task.
Saf. What task?
Sul. We shall know more of it the more we read, so I
believe, but keeping knowledge of the book and
mem'ries of us all alive will fall to thee. For we are
warriors all, prepar'd to give our lives to keep thee free.
Tonight we may be call'd upon to cover thy escape, and
thou in turn must be prepar'd to leave.
Saf. All warriors? thou are not a warrior Keeper.
Keep. I was alive a bit before thee girl.
Sul. It was *Lynette* who taught to me the sword, as she
has taught thee too or so I hear. Thy lessons go so well
she swears that thou art almost ready for the field.

Saf. We play at our conditioning and form, but hardly would I claim to know the arts of war.

Sul. Be that as it may be, it is a skill that one day will be handy. But now must we all trust unto the book my dear, for ev-ery sultina in a thousand years has had a vision of it in their dreams. Though daunting it may seem, I now believe fulfillment of these visions falls to thee.

Saf. Why me?

Sul. Why any child given such responsibility?

Saf. Then I suppose that I should read.

Sul. Our patient ears we lend to thee, a people's savior if thou choose to be.

Saf.

1ˢᵗ day of Henestro, year 334 after the Split.

I have not written in some time, but the events of late lay heavy on mind. Some weeks ago now Toren pick'd a fight with Willimund. It did not go too well for him, or for his friends who tried half-heartedly to help. And now I live in fear that he will want revenge. His eyes burn with an arrogance that only grows the more intense as rumor spread of his alleged miracles. Today we were all oder'd from our homes down to the lake, then told to kneel and pray; but not to all the Thoughts. They now say that the Thoughts are of a sex, all male, and one has risen high above the rest; or always was above the rest, the message changes every day. While we did kneel there not allow'd to raise our heads, then Toren must have paddl'd out into the lake, for when they order'd us to look he did appear to stand upon the water all alone, then quickly we were made to look away.

[*Enter Nebia.*]

I almost laugh'd, though thankfully did not,

[*Shift to past.*]

Neb./Saf. [*Nebia to audience, Safeera still reading.*] (*for I could clearly see he stood upon a board, as on a summer years before by my own father both of us were taught.*)

[*Enter Harat*]

Neb. It's sacrilege! You know that it was fake! The very thoughts themselves may soon descend to protest this disgrace. How can you father-
Har. Keep quiet child! These walls are far too thin.
Neb. What age when lies are forc'd on righteous folk do we live in? The church cannot expect another nation to believe all this?
Har. His reputation grows by day, and pilgrims flock already for an audience with him.
Neb. Surrounded by his handlers I doubt not, who speak for him so he not give away the ruse when his unruly temper grows unduly hot.
Har. It matters not. Our safety is at stake from thy outspoken thoughts. The leaders of the church control the pen, and they are men, so for the sake of peace we must agree with them. They say to pray to him is to absolve thee of all earthly sin, and so we must pretend. What harm is there to quiet stay if by our silence we are sav'd?
Neb. I've seen no evidence that anyone was sav'd, but cast a stone and I'll show thee nearby the grave of one was put there in his name.
Har. Thou knowest what I mean.
Neb. All those who value truth must stand up firm in times like these, that they might stop such lies before they spread from their fictitious seed. How many generations might be plagu'd by these untruthful tales

they weave so cleverly with allegories. Thou art respected father. I know that many men would follow thee if thou would speak up publicly.

Har. To do so'd be to dig my only grave.

Neb. So thou wouldst rather have me be enslav'd? The property of any man the church does choose for me? Thou never treated mother so and she would not have stood it if thou had.

Har. Thou mayst have say in who thou wed if I rise high enough. Already there is talk of privileges for loyalty I've shown. A larger home with land and livestock.

Neb. May *Harat's* livestock live a better life than does his daughter I.

Har. If find I thee a proper man then half the livestock shall be thine.

Neb. They're buying you to help them cover lies.

Har. What other choice have I? To go against them is to die or at the least be banish'd from our home.

Neb. If mother was alive thou would not cower so!

[*Harat slaps her.*]

Har. Nebia…
[*Exit Harat.*]

Neb. (*2ⁿᵈ day of Henestro, year 334 after the Split. I dream'd again today of water far away, a lake surrounded on all sides by trees. Reflection shew a partial sun and two full moons. Some distance to the west beyond the desert sands I feel it call to me.*)

[*Shift to present.*]

Keep. I never thought to hear such heresy, and find myself in league with those who'd bring to light an

ancient institution's insincerity. To think so many could conspire with so few; indeed near ev'ry soul I ever knew.
Sho. Blame not the sheep who spread the word at large; 'tis but the top floor of the ziggurat where stay the wolves in charge.
Pas. The first clan. They take their members from the other clans when they are young, and all are men. It's from these very tyrants in her diary their clan descends.
Sul. It is my clever friend. They pick whichever sultan's wife they wish, and then impregnate them. If that ensuing child is a male, he's taken to the first clan's hold to live; the numbers of the priests are thus replenished.
Saf. The Sultan's simply give the babe away?
Pas. To see them go would serve as a relief I'd say, for most men are possessive of their property, and would not want reminders that a priest had, [*A glance to the Sultina.*] taken liberties. But also it would bind the clans by blood, albeit only through the motherhood.
Sul. Thy guesses all are true, and were confirm'd to me by *Rashtu*, secrets that alone they'd slay us for, regardless of the relic we reliev'd from their most sacred store.
Pash. A system built entirely on lies, block by block and stack'd a mile high.
Sul. Yet were we treated well, no armies at our door, would not we all allow the lies to live forevermore? All systems of control contain their own demise in the corruption at their core.
Saf. May I read more?
Sul. Of course.
Saf.

13th day of Henestro, year 334 after the Split.

My Willimund is under constant scrutiny, and father can do nothing; or chooses to do nothing. Though Toren cannot torment him for now, surrounded by so many worshipers, his friends grow bold and only hold for better opportunity. They will assail him soon. It only is an inquiry of when. If I were brave I would ask Willimund to run away with me unto the lake I see inside my dreams. My fear is not for flight, but whether he would flee with me. I do not know if I can make it on my own.

Keep. The poor girl was as trapp'd as we within our hold.
Saf. So how does she escape?
Sul. How dost thou know she does?
Saf. Was she not first Sultina of our clan?
Sul. Her daughter *Willoselle* was first Sultina,
Who rais'd an army in a hidden hold,
Most female runaways and foreigners,
And all with nowhere else they had to go.
Of *Nebia* though little has been told.
Saf. I know of *Willoselle*, who dug our people in so when the sultans came they could not be dislodg'd, but I must know of *Nebia's* fate ere my fears are assuag'd.
Sul. These pages are the only clue we have.
Saf.

19th day of Henestro, year 334 after the Split.

My father told me Toren has now ask'd for me by name. I know that he would have me for a concubine; already has he tried. Though father swears he can make safe delay, how long until the now thought son of this great male invention in the sky will have his way? Time has expir'd. I will go to my Willimund tonight.

[Shift to past.]

Neb/Saf. [*Nebia to audience, Safeera still reading.*] (If he will not abscond with me, then on my own I shall take flight.) [*Nebia begins to exit, then stops when she sees her father.*]

[Enter Harat.]

Neb. Who are those men who wait outside this time of night?

Har. Forgive me girl.

Neb. I'm just a girl now father, just a girl? Have I no name when it might cause thee shame? No dear one or no darling girl at least? A simple girl, address'd as simply as thy property.

Har. We must unto the church tonight.

Neb. I will not go.

Har. Thou must.

Neb. Then drag me there yet know that I will spit in that false prophet's eye. I shall not ope my legs for *Toren* nor for any churchman lest they hold me down and pry.

Har. It may be that he only wants to speak with thee of marriage, or the possibility.

Neb. Dost think I do not know my childhood friend? Who would have taken 'vantage of our friendship had I never foil'd him? And now with so much power he is nie untouchable, dost think he means to woo me with gentility inside a public vestibule? He has no will to take an honest wife, but only to enslave a pretty thing to see what pleasure and convenience she might bring.

Har. The men outside I told to wait, but they are *Toren's* men and will not leave here empty-handed. My daughter I do not know what they'll do if we do not attend them soon.

Neb. Oh now thy daughter, not a simple girl, when thou fear for thyself and need my help. Had not thou once a sword? Did not thou fight off bandits once who threaten'd us? When I was young and we were on the road, thou stood between them and thy wife and daughter like an angry god. A pillar of the strongest granite thou, unyielding in defense of what thou lov'd. Where is that man *Harat*, that father who would fight for me?

Har. I was that father then.

Neb. Then be that father now, for I have seen thou knowest how. And I shall fight beside thee, for 'twas thee who taught me to protect myself. Take up thy aged blade though rust has riddl'd all it's length, and I shall grab a wooden table leg, or anything that I can use for stabbing or for bludgeoning. Let's raise a cry to wake the town and use this fresh excuse to rouse the crowd. For we are not the only ones who suffer at the hands of these deceptive cultists and their quest for absolute authority. Or if thou fear that we would fall, then let us take them by surprise and flee into the night, to gather strength for when the time to strike is right. I do not fear these men, but I will die before I let them take my freedom.

Har. Thou speakest with the fierceness of thy mother when she pointed out a wrong. Though she is gone, she left thee everything of her inside thyself. I know she would be proud of what thou hast become. Embrace me then before the end.

[*They embrace. Harat will not let go. Nebia struggles to break free.*]

Neb. No father. No! Now let me go!

Har. Forgive me daughter, all of this I do that we might live.

[*He struggles offstage with her as she fights and screams
'no' repeatedly.*]

I have her! Help me with her! Help me!
[*Exit Harat w/ Nebia.*]

Take her from me! Do not hurt her!
***Neb*.** Nooooooo!

[*Shift to present.*]

***Saf*.** [*Thumps the book down.*] I cannot read the end.
***Sul*.** I would not force thee chi-ld to do anything against
thy will. *Pashil*, hie thee to *Rashtu* and return with him,
I'd hear report of any movements by our enemy, and too
require further service from our friend.
***Pas*.** I shall return.
[*Exit Pashil.*]

***Sul*.** I understand that it is difficult to learn such evil
does exist, and I approve thy horror for the worst thing
one can do is learn to live with it. For generations they
have tried unjustly to suppress our will. If we'd prevent
the furtherance of these atrocities, then we must be as
patient and as strong as is an ancient box of steel. And if
thou ever lack for courage, then draw thy strength from
Nebia, for I believe she would have fought those men and
won.
***Saf*.** It simply is not fair to lose a mother thou hast
known, and then a father who has lov'd thee to betray
thee so. I never have known anything but love within the
hold, and no one has betray'd my trust beyond a mi'ld
scolding for not doing something I was told. I was not
forg'd in that same fire as this poor abused girl, so how
can someone such as me find strength to flee when all

that I have known has been so happy and carefree? Just hours gone my only worry was our keeper might allow me not the camel milk to make a custard. What terrors overcome with courage have I known, what strength have I to muster? And thou tell me that I must flee my only home?

Sul. If thou hast not betrayal for a motivation: replace it with necessity. Thou hast no other options for the last of *Nebia's* noble line is thee. Or if betrayal stokes the fire thou wilt need, remember for how long this nation has betray'd thy family.
Since first that day when we became a clan,
A silent war has wag'd beyond the seen,
'Tween sultans who would take from us our land,
And those who tolerate us grudgingly.
But none have ever aided us for free.
O're time enough have raided us at night,
Or us'd the threat of ending all our lives
To take from us what we did own by rights,
That now we have to plunder to survive.
And we are far outnumber'd for to thrive.
Our clan is but a pittance of the force that *Willoselle* once call'd to keep us free, and sultans smell the blood within the water as a fisherwoman smells the sea. So never doubt, my most important sprout, this nation has play'd false with thee.

Saf. The water…

Sul. Yes?

Saf. I too have had some dreams about a lake I've never seen, though they did not seem real to me. Off to the west did she not say? Could it be that there really is a lake?

Sul. I do not know, but what coincidence that thou didst have a dream was written of by *Nebia* herself? It gives me hope that thou may know in which direction thou should go, and from that ancient spring may rise someday a mighty nation bound to no one else. Perhaps she will elaborate if we but read these here remaining lines.

Saf. It is so much to take in such a little time.

Sul. We could not know how swiftly their revenge would come, and thought we would have time enough to fortify and plan to fight or run. I do apologize. And now I see a wounded warrior rises from her needed rest.

[*Enter Shoram, hobbled with pain.*]

Well?

Sho. Sultina, I refuse to die in bed like some old woman who has never held a sword.

Sul. Then sit. We have not time to catch you up on ev'ry word, but thou art sometimes wise and may deduce what went unheard.

Sho. I would insult thee back more apropos, had I the strength,

respected ruler of this hold or no. [*Sits awkwardly, painfully.*].

Sul. [*Places a gentle hand on her arm.*] It brings me joy that thou art here. [*To Safeera.*] If thou cannot continue dear, wilt thou let me pick up where thou left off?

Saf. [*Hands over the book.*] Yes. Please. I do not trust my voice to remain steady while I read.

[*Enter Pashil, Rashtu.*]

Sul. Report.

Pash. They've thrown off any semblance of a peace,
And order'd troops arrang'd in number'd files,
A lookout spied some wooden rams arrive,
Before they cover'd them with shovel'd piles.
This seems to well confirm thy past belief,
As by our trusted spies we have been told,
Nearby was stor'd equipment for a siege,

And plans have been in place to take this hold.
Had we made some delay to snatch the tomb
And stay'd we to behold the tournament,
Regardless of our bold and brazen theft,
They likely would have ambush'd us before we left.
Rash. I can deduce their current line of thought,
For I do know their tactics well as they,
They plan to hand the lion's share of loot
To any clan first sends men 'gainst the gate.
If I would further offer up a guess,
The only thing preventing an attack,
Is squabbling over who is front and back.
Sul. Who didst thou leave in charge of our defense?
Pash. Thy Captain *Analee*.
Sul. Most capable is she. Now *Rashtu* I would ask a special task of thee.
Rash. Whate're thou wish Sultina, cousin, I am yours, though be it to attack the other clans myself, thou hast my loyalty and sword. Thou art the only fam'ly I now know.
Sul. Thou givst me hope, my cousin from a union long ago. I shall inform thee of my wishes momentarily, but first let's see what other wisdom we might gleam from she the spring that first began our lines.
Now sit thee both and listen well.

[Enter Nebia, pregnant.]
Neb.(18th *day of Denastah, year 335 after the Split.*

A cycle of the seasons and near half again has pass'd since my last entry in this book. So much has happen'd since I know not where I should begin. Perhaps I will begin where last I ended then. When Willimund heard rumor of what happen'd he appear'd upon our doorstep in the dead of night. My father, like a fool, arose and open'd it for him; though I am sure that had he not my husband would have made quick work of it. Not husband yet, forgive me if I skip around a bit. He did not murder father, Thoughts be prais'd, though soundly did emasculate him with his tongue, and also toss'd him here and there, but only drew a little blood. I was not of a mind to chastise him, for those were then the darkest moments of my life. The thoughts I had… I will not dwell on them.

We left our village like a pair of thieves who do their work at night that none may see. I wanted to head west to find out if the lake that call'd to me asleep and now awake was real, but Toren's eyes were everywhere along that busy road, so we were forc'd to travel east as far as we could go. My baby girl was born within a weather'd barn, or manger so the owner call'd it; though I think he himself could not define the difference. My Willoselle. My joy. My little one who quickly outgrows all the clothes that we can scavenge for her. We could not stay there long, for that man, I forget his name, became suspicious of our age and sent his son away; likely to inquire if a village miss'd a pair of runaways.

A little longer we remain'd at one almost abandon'd farm, and there did gain a loyal friend who travels with us still, Amallah. Widow'd by a man who long ago had died at war and left her with three daughters and no money, she travell'd with us for the rumor of a long-forgotten hold with running water that could be restor'd. We found the hold and here we stay, with thirteen other, refugees, let's say, we pick'd up on the road along the way.

I know I skipp'd so much, but what I think important is the story of my younger time, a warning to all people who should see the rise of men who prey on faith with promises of favor in the afterlife. Remember always that they fear these words, 'do unto other as thou would have done unto thyself', for once this inborn discipline Is actualiz'd, they have no further wisdom than the most uneducated folk alive; but only half-truths allegories myths and lies.

I threw this journal in the fire once, afraid that Willimund might read it and remember how our Willoselle was sir'd and resent her for it. For she did come from Toren and he knows it in his heart, but never has he spoke of it or show'd a single ounce of anything but love for her. I rescu'd it immediately, sham'd by my impulsiveness when what it stores might one day help so many.

Instead of burning it or letting nature have it's way, my husband, blacksmith that he is, has forged a metal box to keep it from the elements. If thou my kin far down the road have found the key and then the box and open'd it, remember this if thou remember nothing else; men often lie to gain them power sex and wealth.

One final note; I'm pregnant once again. If it's a boy then Willimund says he will one day give the key to him, to pass it down our line for generations, our hope that any women still enslav'd by Toren's story may discover here the truth to end all notions of their obligations to the cult. Our Willoselle will keep the box. Pray never let it fall into the churches hands, or they may burn up half of all humanity as heretics to find the key, and should they ever read these words then all the future come from my most humble seed shall be endangered, and for this risk I pray thou please forgiveth me.)

[Exit Nebia.]

[Shift to present.]

Saf. She liv'd but this was long ago. How did she die? That is what I most long to know.

Sul. There is no record of her death, or even of her life apart from what we have just read. Her name was but a whisper in the wind, a half remember'd murmur on the tongue's inquiring tip.

[*Shouts, distant clash of steel.*]

It has begun. Stand firm! The gates will hold a while yet, and *Analee* shall see that they pay dearly for each step. We four shall more be useful when the gate begins to fail.
Sho. We four?
Sul. A girl alone will gather eyes along the road, so *Rashtu* shall accompany her forth.
A father with his daughter shalt thou be,
Until thou reach the edges of our land,
And cover thee thy face and hair young one,
As do the women in the other clans.
Thou bear the burden of them all this way,
Until thou unmolested find the lake,
Then let these garments of enslavement fall,
For one day thou shalt fight to change their fate.
When thou hast rais'd a power thou shalt send
Thy agents 'mongst the clans of mortal men,
To free those who'd wage war for future days
When none must cover face or hair again.
No more sultinas hiding in their hold,
For lo in my own visions have I seen,
A promise of equality foretold,
The forging of a thought-begotten queen.
We take a form of magic from the book,
For truth is magic stronger than their lies,
One day for all whose freedom was forsook,
False prophets all shall hear our battle cries.
I shall not call my visions prophecy,
For that word has been much abus'd by men,

But know, my girl, that I believe in thee,
And someday from thy able leadership
Our kin will bring a reckoning to them.
A new beginning waits, with freedom for thy people in
the queendom thou shalt make. Take thou this pouch and
hide it well, it holds some gold, and jewelry thou might
someday sell. Thou can'st not make a new begging as a
beggar or a fugitive, I'd give thee more if only I had
more to give.
Saf. Why dost not all of thee accompany? Shall we not
know thy fates until, until we know not when?
Keep. We all of us are sworn to best protect the blood of
Nebia, and willing stay and fight that thou might be
successful in thy flight. Now go my wayward girl, now
go my child who is as I would have my own, now go
until thou find our promis'd land; and do not stop till no
more dost thou see a single grain of sand.
Saf. I shall not think of else but all of thee until we are
together once again!

[Exit Safeera.]

Rash. Thou knowest I would stay.
Sul. Thy part is more important than another death upon
the field. Be on thy way, and let thou nothing foul befall
that girl.
Rash. It was an honor to have serv'd.

[Exit Rashtu.]

Sho. The future's only hope on shoulders of a child and
a man.
Sul. A very special chi-ld, and a man of *Nebia's* line who
long has kept a silent vigil for our clan.
Keep. Yet will she not need guidance at her journey's
end?

Sul. Thou didst not think that mothers so would let their daughter go without a plan to guide her as she grows? The magic is in my blood just as well, and what would be the good of magic if one cannot cast a spell? Wouldst thou all swear an oath to stay thee tether'd to this mortal realm until thou feel our cause has been fulfill'd?
Keep/Sho/Pash. We would.
Sul. I thought as much but would not alter journey of thy souls without thy full consent. (How strange that it is called a miracle when men decide to cast a spell, but when a woman does the same it is supposed that the power comes from some imaginary;) well, give me thy hands.

[*The Sultina, Keeper, Shoram, Pashil hold hands in a circle.*]

A pledge we make unbreakable,
That binds us all to Nebia's line,
Our wisdom from beyond the veil,
To lend until the proper time.
Through water spirits conduit,
Maintain we four a spectral door,
Beginning when we make our end,
Agreed upon by all we four.

The pact is made.
Sho. Now have we not some bloody business to perform?
Sul. [*Draws her sword.*] For our *Cozette,* and all of those who lost their lives before.
Keep. [*Draws her sword.*] To buy our dear *Safeera* time to flee.
Sho. [*Draws her sword.*] Because I shall not die in bed.

Pas. [*Draws her sword*.] For all involuntary who were
forc'd to wed.
Sul. If we should die this day, let's take as many who
would own us with us as we may.
[Exeunt.]

[*A mighty crash. Battle cries. The sound of steel on steel.*]

Act III

[*Enter Safeera, Rashtu.*]
[*Safeera removes the scarf that covers her neck, face,
and hair, kneels before the lake.*]

Saf. Precisely as within the dream this lake appears to
me. Reflected on the surface that same imag'ry. Should
there not be some overwhelming peace? Should not some
sacred wind arise, some breath of those who fought and
died to signal all their souls release?
Rash. Thou art alive and free, as thy fair mother wish'd
for it to be.
Saf. Then why does no triumphant beacon hail her
victory? No songbird celebrates beyond an endless chirp.
No howls of joy from creatures of the earth. No herald
even of a better time foretold. Naught but a queen in only
name who kneels alone, no notion what the future holds.
Rash. In life there never is a guarantee of better times,
but hope can help to see thou art prepar'd when
opportunity arrives. And thou art not alone for thou hast
me, and though a single subject is no mighty army, know
that I would go to any lengths for thee.
Saf. Thou wert a good companion on a long and
treach'rous road, which I might not have navigated safely
on my own. I do not mean to say that thou art none. So I
amend; a queen in only name who kneels by one. But it is
not thy destiny to raise a dynasty, while such of me did
our Sultina ask. The trust of all our people is in me, but
what if I'm inadequate for such a vital task?

Rash. For all my life my cause was kept in secrecy, befriending those who'd kill me if they knew the secret that was my most sacrosanct responsibility. Forever was I destin'd for some great events, or meant to lose the key and with it any chance of our extended family's recompense. If those judicious forces that did long ago foresee, an ancestor of *Nebia* would find the book and hold the key, have chosen thee for their avenging queen, then who am I to speak against the providence I've seen. And these are no uneducated worshippers of doctrine forc'd upon them at an early age who sent us here, but thy Sultina and her peers, enlighten'd women who objectively have liv'd outside the mindset of the cult for years. Thou art of that most open-minded seed, and so I think to fail against the patriarchy's not thy destiny.

Saf. Those women now are likely dead, made sacrifice that I might be here in their stead; and yet I feel no different. No answers come to me in wakefulness or dreams, nor visions light my pathway in the night by moon-derived beams. That I might forge an empire to wage a war against all inequality? If thou art here my ancestors, please send a sign to me. [*When nothing happens, she rises*.] I won't believe we came so far in vain. Not yet. But little does my hope remain. [*She begins to exit*].

Ras. Perhaps a humor-laden anecdote would raise the spirits and provide thee hope?

Saf. I'm listening.

Ras. A clergyman, a warrior, and a monkey were once forc'd to share a wayside tent. The clergyman was last to enter, darkness falling and his breathing spent. 'There's brigands hereabout', the holy man proclaim'd. The monkey shriek'd [*Makes monkey sounds*.], the warrior grunted and began to draw his blade. 'No need for that, my son,' the clergyman assur'd. If thou but give to me

thy gold then rest assur'd, the great male thought shall keep me safe, and I shall see the bandits are deterr'd. The warrior grumbl'd but he gave the man the gold. The monkey shriek'd again [*Makes monkey sounds.*] The clergyman he wink'd, then disappear'd beyond the outer fold. The monkey and the warrior waited most impatiently, until the warrior could not wait another beat, and so pull'd back the flap himself to see what he could see. There were no brigands nor a clergyman, and only one new set up footprints led away into the darkness and the sand. The monkey laugh'd, then shook his head and clear'd his throat to speak. 'I tried to tell thee that the churchman was the brigand, you metal-minded mental miniature.' The warrior just stood dumbfounded. The monkey frown'd and ask'd, 'art thou in shock to hear a monkey talk'? To that replied the warrior, 'nay monkey, tis but my first encounter with an honest clergyman'!
Saf. That was the longest-winded winding tale I've ever heard unfold, much more enjoy'd I take it by the teller than the told.

[*Enter spirit of Cossania.*]
Cos. *Safeera.*
Saf. What mournful maiden of the mist arises from the lake to coalesce as though in form a frosty breath?
Cos. Didst doubt dear child thy kin would care for thee in death?
Saf. How can this be?

[*Enter spirit of Lynette.*]
Lyn. We watch and wait in timeless wakefulness. That we might give thee warning darling girl, when secrets find we from this netherworld.
Saf. What happen'd at the siege?

[Enter spirits of Shoram, Pahil.]

Sho. The sultans' men did crash upon our hold in waves, and broke like waves are want to do when rock is what they crash into.

Pash. They ended their assault when first that morning sun did rise, assumingly assessing further cost in human lives.

Cos. Though took we nowhere near the toll as they, our numbers were as wagons are to hay. Some little more than fifty of our warriors yet remain, for we've not felt them pass beyond thy earthly plain. Their orders are to jo-in thee in twos and threes, with faces cover'd to outwit the enemy, and pris'ners at a dagger's point to lead, a motivated man for each, with promise of continu'd health if our new queen they safely reach.

Saf. But thou art not among them for I felt a chill at first thy sight, and still it grows within my bones despite the dawning light.

Cos. To speak across the veil does cost the living and the dead, on only rare occasion should it even be attempted. Yet thou and thy descendants all may find us in thy times of greatest need, so long as they are strong enough and born of *Nebia's* seed. And if we do deduce some danger we would warn thee of, we'll send a signal to a single sprout of *Nebia's* blood, that they may come to gaze upon the lake and take what wisdom they would take, from we who watch and wait, bespying from a place where past and future are the same for all our people's sake.

Saf. Though I grow cold thou bring me comfort mothers, all of thee are mothers to me now.

Lyn. And always will be daughter who I raised.

Cos. Oh daughter who I bore.

Pas. Oh daughter who I taught to hunt.

Sho. Oh daughter who I chase'd through countless halls for sneaking pastries after dark.

Sul. We tarry far too long and cannot stay, before our presence causes further harm we must away.
Lyn/Cos/Pas/Sho. [*As they back away*]. Fear not for thou shalt never be alone, we keep a constant vigil on the world from the unknown.
>[*Exeunt, manet Cossania, Safeera, Rashtu.*]

Saf. But stay! How shall I know what course to take will best maintain our freedom?
Sul. Thoult know. Thy heart and mind are everything thou need to raise a queendom.
Saf. If thou say so I will no longer doubt, but try and trust myself to choose the truest route.
Cos. What wilt thou name thy queendom fated one?
Saf. The image of the moons in concert with the partly risen sun came to me as reflected in a mirror at the dawn, so I shall call it… *Myradawn*.
Cos. Thou always were a special sprout, and thou shalt make a conscientious queen, of that I have no doubt. Farewell… for now.
>[*Exit spirit of Cossania.*]

Rash. [*Feels at himself.*] We are not in the spirit world? We have not died? My breath no longer frosted indicates we are alive.
Saf. Thy eyes perceiv'd them as did mine? Four ghostly figures that we knew in life?
Rash. And heard them too, though did not dare to speak. I felt their otherworldly wisdom was not meant for me.
Saf. I'm thankful to the thoughts thou wert a witness to this unexpected spectral visitation. Although I strong suspected it was no hallucination, thy words confirm to me that it was not imagination.
Rash. This truly is a wonder we have witness'd. If I should die this day I should consider myself bless'd.

Saf. Thou art of *Nebia's* blood thyself, and I could not have come so far without thy strong support. Thou canst not die, for I command that thou forever hold a place of honor in my court. Dost thou not re'lize uncle thou art now my only living fam'ly in the world?

Rash. Thou hast a fam'ly here within the lake, with many friends and warlike maidens on the way. Still others they will want to jo-in us when once they do perceive thy righteous cause.

Saf. 'Tis true enough, each point thou make.

Rash. What is it then that brings thee pause?

Saf. I only wish that *Nebia* had made it to her lake.
    [*Enter spirit of Nebia, lingers near edge of stage with a smile.*]

What now to raise our spirits shall we do?

Rash. [*Laughs*.] Thou art a queen, whose word I'd rate holds greater weight than even a sultina; I shall follow you.

Saf. Then let us find a proper clearing in these woods to wait for those who come to join our ranks. Along the way we'll hunt, and have a feast awaiting them when they arrive to gain their thanks. I've seen so many tracks, and it is rich and fertile soil, most certain we will find some meat or berries, maybe roots to boil. How does that sound sir knight?

Rash. A knight?

Saf. Should not a queen have knights as western kings will do?

Rash. So I suppose.

Saf. Good. Dost think these woods have hens and camels knight, to give us eggs and milk?

Rash. Wild fowl would give us eggs, and goats or donkeys, maybe cows for milk.

Saf. Be on the lookout for these beasts, whilst I obtain some cuttings from the many maples I have seen to boil down for sugar sweet. I have what little gold was given me that we might gain a footing here. A village with a market must be near. We'll need some salt and flour too…

Rash. Might I inquire what thou dost intend to do?

Saf. What weary warrior would not want a custard waiting after waging war and walking o'er so many miles of sand? I will not be a queen who greets her people with an empty hand.

Rash. As my Sultina; forgive me. Thy knight is at his queen's command.

Saf. Accompany me then.

[*Exeunt.*]

FINIS

PUNCTUATION GUIDELINES

[Based on Original Practice Shakespeare guidelines, for use with all J.L. Davis Original Practice plays.]

Comma=Half stop w/ breath.
Period=Full stop w/ breath. [Mid-line periods in lines of verse should not be treated as a stop.]
Question mark=Full stop w/ breath. [Mid-line question mark in lines of verse should not be treated as a stop.]
Colon=Briefly speed up. [As if to hold someone's attention, not be interrupted, or excited about a new thought.]
Semicolon=Distinct change in thought. [Breath optional.]
Parenthesis=Suggests delivery to audience. [Many other lines may also be played to audience.]

GENERAL NOTES

The iambic rhythm is essential for this play. It is the 'heartbeat' of each character and each character's heartbeat is unique. Together, the heartbeats equal the heartbeat of the play, and as with all living things if the heartbeat stops, the play… dies. The rhythm can almost always be easily found by stressing the second syllable of each line. If a line is not written in iambic, there is a reason ['Real-talk' asides to audience, character is flustered, etc.*]

*Most lines rhyme. It is up to the performer to choose which rhymes are important to emphasize and which should be played down to avoid the language becoming sing-songy.

*If every line of an extended paragraph begins with a capitol letter, it is verse. [*Most verse lines will have 10 beats, soft endings will have 11.*]. If not, it is prose. There are many reasons a character may switch from verse to prose or vice versa, often within a single monologue. It is usually a simple change in emotion or tactic, but it is very important to find, or create, that reason for yourself when reading/performing the character.

*Words that end in 'ed' always receive a separate beat for the 'ed', but words that naturally receive a separate beat for an 'ed' ending do not receive an extra beat.

*Words that contain a non-possessive apostrophe are truncated, or contracted, removing a beat or beats. [*Example: Possessed=3 beats. Possess'd=2 beats.*]

*The fourth wall does not exist. The audience should be treated as a member of the cast as long as they, as a whole and/or individually, do not become uncomfortable. Excessive commotions in the audience should by tactfully acknowledged and perhaps remarked on in character and treated as part of the show. The same is true of excessive disturbances. The idea, as always, is to pull the audience into the world of the play and keep them there. If they wish to be completely ignored by performers, they most assuredly have a television at home.

Mahalo!

Other Plays by J.L Davis:
The Dragon's Tooth
Myradawn
Witch Queen of the Isle
Little Birds

Novels by J.L. Davis:
Fall of Crysin (Book I of the Irrillania Chronicles)
Ashes of Crysin (Book II of the Irrillania Chronicles)

Coming soon:
Blood of Crysin (Book III of the Irrillania Chronicles)
Iambic Rambleameter (Scenes and monologues)
Threads (A heightened language play)
Evidence Room (A play)

About the author:
J.L. Davis is a novelist, playwright, and stage performer
who graduated from Pacific Lutheran University with a
BFA in acting.

www.ingramcontent.com/pod-product-compliance
Lightning Source LLC
Chambersburg PA
CBHW071511130726
47997CB00006B/2490